Reading Gems

FACT FINDERS

Koalas

Quarto is the authority on a wide range of topics.

Quarto educates, entertains and enriches the lives of our readers—enthusiasts and lovers of hands-on living.

www.quartoknows.com

Author: Katie Woolley
Series Editor: Joyce Bentley
Series Designer: Jo Garden
Topic consultant: Michael Bright

© 2019 Quarto Publishing plc

First published in 2019 by QED Publishing,
an imprint of The Quarto Group.
The Old Brewery, 6 Blundell Street,
London N7 9BH, United Kingdom.
T (0)20 7700 6700 F (0)20 7700 8066
www.QuartoKnows.com

A catalogue record for this book is
available from the British Library.

ISBN 978-0-7112-4379-8

Manufactured in Shenzhen, China PP05201
9 8 7 6 5 4 3 2 1

MIX
Paper from
responsible sources
FSC® C001701

Photo Acknowledgments
Nature Picture Library: p14-15 Rolan Seitre
/ naturepl.com; 22 Larent Geslin / naturepl.
com; p23 and 25 Suzi Eszterhas / naturepl.
com; **Shutterstock**: front cover, back cover
imprint page, p8 and 25 Eric Isselee; title
page TRossJones; page 4 Roberto La Rosa;
page 5 and 24 Olga Utchenko; p6 Yatra;
p7 and 24 1989studio; p9 and 24 Jed R;
p10 Raffaella Simonchi; p11 and 24 John
Carnemolla; p12 and 24 Poramate Pilay; p1
and 25 iofoto; p16-17 and 24 apple2499; p18
and 24 Henri Faure; p19 and 24 Wonderly
Imaging; p20, 24 and 25 Wonderly Imagir
p21 Mark Higgins;

Contents

In Australia

Koalas are furry animals.

They live in Australia.

Australia

Koala Looks

Koalas have big noses
and big ears.

ear

nose

They have sharp claws.

claws

Koala Fur

Koalas have grey and white fur.

grey fur

white fur

The fur keeps the koala dry
in the rain.

In the Trees

Koalas live in the trees.
They sleep a lot.

Koala Food

Koalas eat lots of eucalyptus leaves.

eucalyptus
(yoo-ca-lip-tus)
leaves

All Alone

Koalas live alone in the trees.

Baby Koalas

A baby koala is a joey.

joey

Koala Pouch

A mother looks after a joey.
She has a pouch.

mother

The joey lives in it.

pouch

Nocturnal Animals

Koalas are nocturnal.
They are awake at night.

They need to sleep all day.

Wild Koalas

Koalas live in the wild.

We need to look after the trees they live in.

Picture Glossary

Australia

awake

claws

dry

eucalyptus tree

food

grey fur

leaves

mother

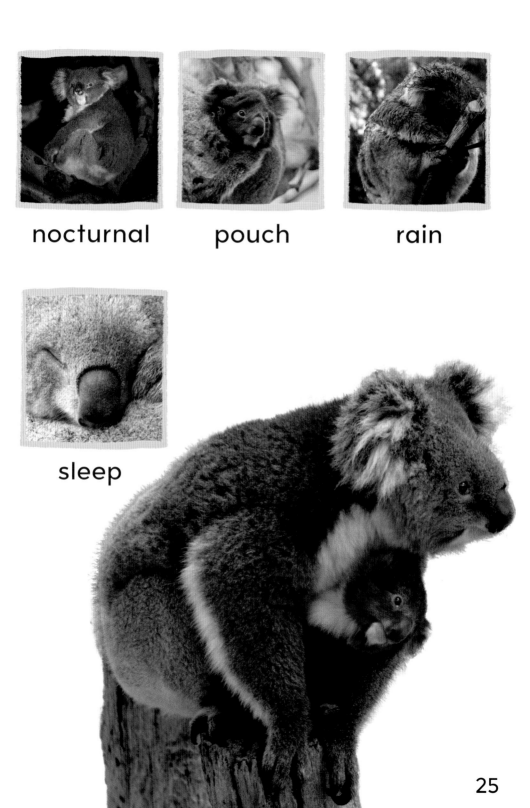

nocturnal

pouch

rain

sleep

Let's Talk About Koalas!

Look at the book cover.

What colour is the koala?

Does it have big ears?

What other features of a koala can you see? (e.g. small eyes, big nose)

Where do koalas live?

Can you think of three words to describe a koala's habitat?

Can you tell me a sentence about koalas?

Koalas are nocturnal. This means they are awake at night.

What do koalas do in the day?

What other animals are nocturnal?

Koalas are wild animals.

They live in trees in Australia.

What special leaves do they like to eat?

What other animals live only in Australia?

Draw a picture of a koala.

Can you label its body parts?

Fun and Games

Match these words to the pictures below

sleep

big ears

joey

leaves

a

b

c

d

Answer a: sleep; b: joey; c: leaves and d: big ears.

Look at this picture. Can you answer these questions about koalas?

1. Do you like koalas?

2. What do you like or not like about them?

3. If you were a koala for a day, what would you do?

Koala Quiz

What can you remember about koalas?
Which of these statements are true
and which are false?

1. Koalas live in Australia.

2. Koalas have green fur.

3. Koalas sleep all day.

4. Koalas are not wild animals.

5. Koalas have small ears and small noses.

6. Koalas live in groups.

7. Koalas eat corn.

8. We need to look after eucalyptus trees.

GET TO KNOW READING GEMS

Reading Gems is a series of books that has been written for children who are learning to read. The books have been created in consultation with a literacy specialist.

The books fit into five levels, with each level getting more challenging as a child's confidence and reading ability grows. The simple text and fun photos provide gradual, structured practice of reading. Most importantly, these books are good accounts that are fun to read!

Phonics is for children who are learning their letters and sounds. Simple, engaging stories provide gentle phonics practice.

Level 1 is for children who are taking their first steps into reading. Story themes and non-fiction subjects are familiar to children, and there is lots of repetition to build reading confidence.

Level 2 is for children who have taken their first reading steps and are becoming readers. Story themes are still familiar but sentences are a bit longer, as children begin to tackle more challenging vocabulary.

Level 3 is for children who are developing as readers. Stories and subjects are varied, and more descriptive words are introduced.

Level 4 is for readers who are rapidly growing in reading confidence and independence. There is less repetition on the page, broader themes are explored and plot lines straddle multiple pages.

Level 1

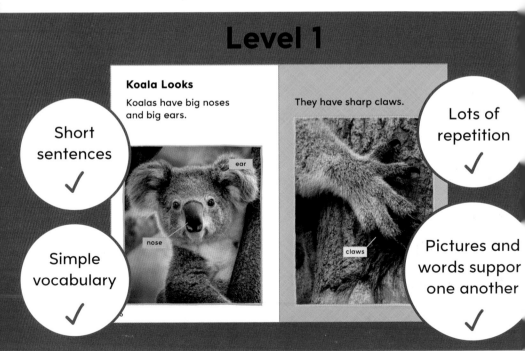

Koala Looks
Koalas have big noses and big ears.

ear

nose

They have sharp claws.

claws

Short sentences ✓

Lots of repetition ✓

Simple vocabulary ✓

Pictures and words support one another ✓

32